Glimpses

An Artistic Perspective on Humber

Edited by **Michael J. Hatton**

Watercolours by **Bogumila Derewicz** and **Daniela Molina**

Library and Archives Canada Cataloguing in Publication

Glimpses : an artistic perspective on Humber / edited by
Michael J. Hatton ; watercolors by Bogumila Derewicz and
Daniela Molina.

ISBN 978-0-9734977-1-7

1. Humber Institute of Technology & Advanced Learning--
Buildings--Pictorial works. I. Hatton, Michael J. (Michael John), 1948-
II. Derewicz, Bogumila, 1959- III. Molina, Daniela, 1988-

LE3.H873G55 2012   378.713'541   C2012-907349-0

Prose and Photographs by
    Michael Hatton   email: michael.hatton@humber.ca

Watercolours by
    Bogumila Derewicz   email: bogumila.derewicz@gmail.com
    Daniela Molina   email: molinas.daniela@gmail.com

Creative Direction by
    James Hickman   email: jim@manxcreative.com

Planning and Logistics by
    Nancy Rodrigues   email: nancy.rodrigues@humber.ca

PRINTED IN CANADA

Humber Press 2012

Welcome to Glimpses...

and to Humber, one of Canada's largest, most comprehensive polytechnics. Well known for professional programs in business, health, media, social services and technology, the institute is also home to strong and vibrant arts programs.

Humber is a large institution with eclectic architecture – old and new, traditional red brick alongside steel and glass, single and multi-storey, one campus near the hustle and bustle of the airport, while the other sits on the shore of Lake Ontario.

In *Glimpses* you'll see how the two main campuses, and the contrasts they represent, are perceived by student watercolourists from Humber's visual arts programs. We hope that, in addition to looking through these pages, you will walk the grounds personally to create your own interpretation of Humber.

With best wishes,

Michael J. Hatton
Vice President Academic
Humber Institute

Modernist concrete, steel and glass...

showcase classrooms and design and technology labs at the North Campus buildings. Perhaps most relevant is the use of windows, with most lecture halls, laboratories and offices looking out on the world.

A favourite area...

during the warmest months is the grass and glass in front of E Building. The mother and child sculpture has witnessed more than four decades of students.

Behind the main "wall"...

of the North Campus lies a student
amphitheatre, a site for various events,
including concerts, orientation programs,
barbecues and informal socializing.

HSF
amphitheatre

At both campuses...

a variety of meeting areas, art and artifacts reminds students of the area's heritage. Here you'll find bark canoes and paintings from the aboriginal community.

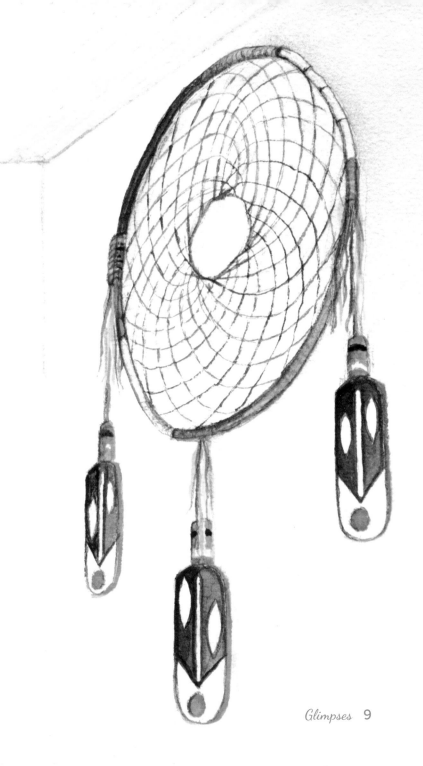

Adjoining the North Campus...

the 250-acre Humber Arboretum displays an extensive and growing collection of woody and herbaceous plants. Also prevalent are many animals that create the full circle of life in this natural habitat.

Resting on the side...

of a small hill just inside the Arboretum is the Centre for Urban Ecology. This building is Gold LEED® (Leadership in Energy and Environmental Design) certified, as well as Platinum-certified as an Ontario Ecocentre.

The shift from...

the North Campus (left) to the
Lakeshore Campus (right) is
dramatic. From newer to older,
from larger to smaller, the
architectural differences create
an exciting change.

Although there are…

many buildings – and building types – at Lakeshore, the campus is best known for older "red-brick" buildings that combine Neo-Gothic, Romanesque Revival and contemporary layers into their design.

Nestled on the shore...

of Lake Ontario, the original buildings opened in 1890 as a psychiatric hospital. It was designed to accommodate patients who, it was thought, might benefit from a more open architecture and a smaller patient-to-doctor ratio.

Sitting in the midst...

of the ruddy-hued buildings is something new: a taller, white brick and glass structure that was specifically designed to complement the older structures. L Building is home to specialized classrooms, laboratories and an art gallery.

With easy access, low height...

and a welcoming portico, this former hospital
site now hosts media students specializing
in journalism, advertising, public relations
and various other arts programs.

Romanesque architecture…

is easily identified by round arches, thick walls and strong columns. Its symmetry and simple nature – contrasted by the later Neo-Gothic style – is clearly visible at Lakeshore.

Originally a destination...

for patients who at that time were described as "insane" but thought to be "curable," the dim, cold corridors running underground from building to building are often cited as places where voices from long ago can be faintly heard.

While buildings often dominate…

the artists' brushes, Humber is about people, and students in particular. Classes tend to be small, faculty members are everywhere, academic and applied subjects are diverse, and graduates are well prepared.

At the heart of Humber...

is formal and informal learning. With almost 30,000 students from more than 100 countries, the opportunity to glean knowledge with – and from – others is ever present.